SCOTT FRANCIS

EXAM SKILLS HANDBOOK

How to Study and Perform Better in Exams

Acknowledgements

With sincere thanks to my parents, Wendy and Paul, who encouraged and supported me in an infinite number of ways, including in my own studies and later with my work as a teacher.

Published in 2024 by Amba Press, Melbourne, Australia
www.ambapress.com.au

© Scott Francis 2024

All rights reserved. No part of this book may be reproduced or transmitted in any form or by any means, electronic or mechanical, including photocopying, recording or by any information storage and retrieval system, without prior permission in writing from the publisher.

Cover design: Tess McCabe
Editor: Rica Dearman

ISBN: 9781923116634 (pbk)
ISBN: 9781923116641 (ebk)

A catalogue record for this book is available from the National Library of Australia.

Contents

Introduction – Your tools: The eight superhabits of study		1
Chapter 1	Stage 1: Being effective early – before the first class	9
Chapter 2	Stage 2: Making term time count	21
Chapter 3	Stage 3: Taking advantage of SWOTVAC and exam block	37
Chapter 4	Stage 4: The 24 hours before an exam	57
Chapter 5	Stage 5: Building an exam routine	63
Chapter 6	Stage 6: Feedback and reflection	73
Chapter 7	The challenge of procrastination	77
References		83

Introduction – Your tools: The eight superhabits of study

Ever since I started teaching, I have had an interest in how study and study skills work.

As much as I was interested in the ideas around study skills, I quickly learned that students tend to be far less interested. That posed a challenge for me – how could I communicate the key information on a topic that was of interest to me and important to learning?

The answer to my challenge was an infographic. I wanted to see if I could get the most important information about the elements that impact study into one image. That led to a lot of thinking.

The first step was the idea that study is impacted by 'superhabits' – 'habits' because they can be controlled by the student, and 'super' because they have the biggest impact. These superhabits range from getting enough sleep to using practice tests/questions.

Alongside this concept are two key ideas:

The first is to challenge the often-cited measurement of study as time. For example, you might hear a student say, "I did so much study on the weekend, I spent 10 hours finishing an assignment and revising for an exam". That tells you very little about how much they actually got done.

Perhaps they went to the library, studied largely in silence, had regular breaks of five minutes to refresh their thinking, set goals for smaller blocks of time and did an impressive amount of work.

Or...

Perhaps they lay on their bed with two screens open on the laptop, switched between social media and study, and watched YouTube videos of cats being scared of cucumbers on their iPad and got very little study done.

That is why the eight superhabits of study image has the formula that focuses on the study impact, what actually gets done. The formula is: **study impact = intensity of effort × time**. A lot of the ideas in this book, from studying without distractions to using practice questions to test what you know, are about the intensity of your effort while you study.

The second idea is one that is important to me: **life is too good for bad study**. There are so many good things in the world – family, friends, music, sport, nature, galleries, art – so when you make the effort to sit down and study, do it well. If you are going to forego those good things for a while, then honour the commitment you have made by working well. After all, for most of us, life is too good for bad study.

Opposite is the image of the eight superhabits of study, which contains a summary of what I think are the best study ideas:

In this book you will read about six stages of exam study, but before we launch into those, I want to introduce each of the eight superhabits to you. They will be explained in more detail throughout the book, along with some of the research that supports the importance of each superhabit to study and learning.

Superhabit of sleep – Eight to 10 hours of sleep at night, as often as possible, will make you a better and happier learner. Important consolidation of learning and preparation for learning happens during sleep. Great sleep is a superhabit that supports great learning.

Superhabit of A+ effort in class – Your class time is where you have the most concentrated learning resources (teacher, textbooks, peers, laptop, online resources) in a low-distraction environment. It is also where, for most people, important knowledge and skills are first encountered. Getting the most out of class is a superhabit that sets a foundation for good results.

Superhabit of setting goals – Goals can be a useful tool to help focus effort. Taking the time to thoughtfully set and revise goals, as well as thinking about the actions needed to work toward them, is a superhabit that supports student performance.

Superhabit of single-tasking – The idea that 'digital distractions' follow us everywhere is no longer a profound observation – it is a well-known reality. These digital distractions – devices, social media, screens – alongside real-life distractions make study hard. If you can develop the superhabit of single-tasking, working without distraction for periods of time, you put yourself in a strong position to learn.

Superhabit of planning and to-do lists – Some research suggests that our brain spends a certain amount of energy focusing on the distraction of what needs to be done in the future. For example, the big accounting assignment due in two weeks is something we might be worrying about during an English class. However, if we have a plan that sets out when we can work on different subjects each week (including accounting), and a to-do list showing what we need to do (including tasks for the accounting assignment), that background worrying is lessened, making the superhabit of planning and a to-do list a useful one.

Superhabit of a deliberate mindset – We can choose our attitude in a lot of situations, and this is behind the idea of a deliberate mindset. For example, with challenging work, we can decide to give up, or we can decide to persist with it because we know it will build capacity. Equally, when we have a hard choice – perhaps in the week before an exam, choosing between an evening at the movies or some extra study – we can decide who we want to be. A deliberate mindset is a superhabit that we can use to nudge our attitude and actions.

Superhabit of starting early (spaced practice) – Cramming is a well-known study approach. It is a high-pressure strategy with limited benefits, as tired students struggle to make the most of 'the last minute' to cobble together some learning to drag into the exam with them. Starting early and revising regularly (which the research refers to as 'spaced practice' or 'distributed practice') takes no longer than cramming, and is more effective with less stress, making starting early an important superhabit for students to access.

Superhabit of practice tests/questions – This superhabit encourages students to practise answering questions about the content they have covered. This is an effective way of revising regularly, and provides great feedback on what is known and what still has to be learnt. 'Flashcards' with questions on one side and answers on the other have been known to be a productive way of learning over many years. The superhabit of practice tests/questions shows these students have been on the right path.

The next step is to look at how we can use these superhabits along with other study strategies to help prepare us to be our best on exam day. As these superhabits and study strategies are introduced throughout the six stages of exam study, you might consider them on the basis of, 'What is the price I am prepared to pay?' They all take time and effort, and won't be for everyone. But as you come across each strategy, you might find that deciding whether this is a price you are prepared to pay, to build a better study routine, is an interesting way of challenging yourself to take action.

> ### Learning from students
>
> While there will be a variety of research used throughout this book, I will also use pieces of feedback that comes directly from students.
>
> To start with, some time ago, I asked secondary students who were averaging an 'A' grade point average (GPA) how important their study was to their success compared to their work in class.
>
> Of these successful students, 76.4% said that study was equally or more important than the time they spent in class.
>
> If study is that important to successful students, it follows that it is worth having a plan to study effectively, which is the basis of this book.

Within each of the six stages of exam study in this book, you will find information on the eight superhabits and some additional study strategies, along with how they can help you. Each of these stages is broken into the following sections:

The key aims of... – this is an introduction to the main aims of each stage.

Study superhabits for you to use – this section incorporates the superhabits that are relevant for each stage as well as some additional study strategies, which contain some practical tools to help you study.

Putting things into practice – here you will find out how you can use the superhabits and study strategies mentioned in the previous section.

The takeaway message – this is a summary of how the superhabits and study strategies can help you.

Here are the six stages of exam study:

Stage 1:	Stage 2:	Stage 3:	Stage 4:	Stage 5:	Stage 6:
Before the first class	Classes are on (supported by study)	SWOTVAC and exam block	24 hours before an exam	An exam routine	Feedback and reflection

CHAPTER 1

Stage 1: Being effective early – before the first class

"What would life be if we had no courage to attempt anything?"

Vincent van Gogh (Dutch Post-Impressionist painter)

Stage 1: Before the first class	Stage 2: Classes are on (supported by study)	Stage 3: SWOTVAC and exam block	Stage 4: 24 hours before an exam	Stage 5: An exam routine	Stage 6: Feedback and reflection

The key aims of being effective early

Being effective early – even before the first class – is about 1) organisation; and 2) previewing content. Being well organised, with some understanding of the upcoming subject matter, puts you in the best position for success.

The organisational element includes having the resources ready to be effective from the first class, as well as a weekly planner in place and a to-do list ready so that, as important tasks become pressing, there is a system in place to deal with them.

The previewing element allows you exposure to the content before the first class. As we will see as we come to understand the superhabit of starting early, repeated exposure to material over time helps build the ability to recall it.

As well as getting organised and previewing content, it is a great time to use the superhabit of setting a goal, to set a clear intent for your work.

Study superhabits for you to use

The superhabits that will help you in being effective early include:

Superhabit of setting goals
Superhabit of planning and to-do lists
Superhabit of starting early (and spaced practice)

Superhabit of setting goals

The first superhabit we will talk about in Stage 1 is the superhabit of setting goals, which is a great starting point for any academic challenge. The idea behind setting a goal is relatively simple: goals can help drive effort in a desired direction. We often hear about athletes, musicians and business leaders who use goals to positively influence their performance. Study is a high-performance activity that requires effort, sacrifice, dedication, improvement and reflection, so having this supported through the use of goals makes sense.

One of the foremost researchers on the impact of goals is Edwin Locke, who found that the impact of setting goals on performance across a range of situations is reliable and positive (Locke, 2002).

I want to propose two types of goal setting. The first is generally well known: setting a 'SMART' goal. SMART stands for a goal that is:

Specific
Measurable
Achievable through actions
Realistic
Timebound

And I like to include '**R**eflection' as the final step of setting a goal.

So, a **SMART'R** goal to do well in a subject, let's say Psychology, might look like this:

Specific	I want to improve my Psychology result from 72% to 82% this semester
Measurable	The mark will increase from 72% to 82%
Achievable through actions	I will: • Attend all classes • Spend 10 minutes reading ahead each week • Create a mind map of topics covered each week • Start revising for the exam at the start of exam block
Realistic	A 10% increase in a result is challenging, but possible (and challenging goals are great!)
Timebound	It happens over this term
Reflection	After each draft, assessment task and practice test, I will see what I can learn about my progress

SMART goals have been around for a long time; I remember visiting the Australian Institute of Sport 20 years ago and it was using SMART goals with athletes then.

Australian researcher Dr Christian Swann (2021) has looked at the idea of setting 'open goals' rather than SMART goals. Instead of setting a specific performance goal, an open goal encourages people to see how much they can improve. Much of Dr Swann's research is based on the use of goals for exercise. So, rather than setting a specific goal of walking 10,000 steps per day, an open goal might be to 'see how far I can walk each day'. An open goal is non-specific (different to the 'S' in SMART goals) and exploratory. Dr Swann's research has suggested that the performance increase from a SMART or open goal is similar, with open goals being more enjoyable and leading to greater confidence.

SMART goals are also very 'all or nothing'. Consider the student looking to improve a Psychology result from 72% to 82%. An 80% result is a failure based on a SMART goal, while in reality it is an impressive result. That same increase based on an open goal is easier to acknowledge as a success and might be more enjoyable.

Putting your open or SMART goal in writing, to make your intent concrete, seems to improve results.

Learning from students

I was lucky enough, in a school I was working in, to put together a survey that was sent to the students who had improved their average result the most over a year. I was interested in what they might say were the reasons behind their success.

Of these 'big improvers', 78.3% said they started out with a goal or objective to improve.

If goal setting works as part of the plan for these students, it is worth considering as a study strategy.

Superhabit of planning and to-do lists

Planning and to-do lists seem like relatively simple ideas, but there is surprising sophistication behind them.

Researchers Masicampo and Baumeister (2011) found that when people had a plan toward a goal, they did not spend as much time worrying about how they would meet the goal – they just focused on the goal when they were directly working on it.

Let's think about what this might mean in practice. If you have a large assignment in a subject, it is natural that you might be concerned about how you are going to complete it. In fact, worrying about how you are going to do the assignment might negatively impact your concentration in other classes.

However, if you have a plan on how to complete the assignment, Masicampo and Baumeister (2011) suggest the worry will affect you less – and this is how a weekly planner and to-do list can help. A weekly planner will enable you to know *when* you have time to work on your assignment, and a to-do list shows you *what* you have to do.

Superhabit of starting early (and spaced practice)

Spaced practice is also known as distributed practice in research on learning. Spaced practice is the opposite of 'cramming', where students leave their study until the night before an exam, which can be a stressful experience. Spaced practice is about revising material at a number of different times over the term, semester or year. This more frequent revision improves our ability to recall the material even if the total time spent revising is the same amount of time spent cramming the night before an exam.

An article titled 'Spaced practice and its role in supporting learning and retention' by Dr Efrat Furst, written for the Education Hub in New Zealand (2021), considers some of the key research on this topic. It suggests revising content or skill between one day and one month after it is first learned as an effective spacing interval. For now, starting the term, semester or year, the important step is to consider whether you are prepared to commit to more regular revision of content to improve your learning and reduce the stress of last-minute cramming sessions.

Remember the challenge: what is the price you are prepared to pay?

Putting things into practice

Now that you've learned about three superhabits that can be utilised in this stage of being effective early, let's put these into place in practice.

There are three things that you can do before the start of the term, semester or year that will help your learning.

Set a goal. You may want to set a SMART goal or an open goal (for example, 'I am going to do as well as I can in the subject _____'), and set out the steps you are prepared to take regularly to support success. Either way, there is power in writing down your goal. Mark Murphy, CEO of Leadership IQ, writing for *Forbes* in 2018, discussed the benefits of writing down goals, to remind readers that written items are better remembered and, in the case of goals, 1.2–1.4 times more likely to be accomplished. The total time it takes to do this task is around 15 minutes.

Use a weekly planner and to-do list. The weekly planner can be as simple as a table that includes each day of the week and times during the day, as set out opposite. This is easy enough to create in a Word or Excel document, and you might include a space for your goals.

	Monday	Tuesday	Wednesday	Thursday	Friday	Saturday	Sunday
7am							
8am							
9am							
10am							
11am							
Midday							
1pm							
2pm							
3pm							
4pm							
5pm							
6pm							
7pm							
8pm							
9pm							
9.30pm	Technology free	Technology free	Technology free	Technology free			Technology free
10pm	SLEEP	SLEEP	SLEEP	SLEEP			SLEEP

In a 2015 TED talk about what top students do differently to others, Douglas Barton spoke about the fact that many students write down a weekly planner/study timetable, but very few stick to it over time, some throwing it out in just days. However, the successful students *did* use the planner over time, and they started by putting enjoyable non-study activities into their timetable: time for socialising, hobbies, sport and work. Then they put in their study commitments. Having fun activities in your planner makes it easier to stick to. Like goal setting, this task will take around 15 minutes.

Setting up a to-do list is equally easy. Coach, speaker and author Sarah Davis (2020) suggests that one positive of using to-do lists is that 'ticking off' a finished task gives our brain a little hit of the feel-good chemical dopamine as we see our progress.

Louise Chunn (2017) lists three benefits of a to-do list:

1. They 'dampen anxiety about the chaos of life'
2. They provide structure
3. They show progress as tasks are ticked off

Setting up a to-do list should only take five to 10 minutes and can easily be done with an online template, as a Word or Excel document, or even drawn up on a piece of paper. It could look a little bit like the following table, which allows you to set out tasks, add some comments, set up a date and, importantly, record when a task is complete:

Task	Comments	Finishing date	Complete
Maths homework	Chapter 2, odd number questions	2 December	DONE!
Physics research	Aim to find eight articles related to the topic	3 December	DONE!
English story	Complete draft	8 December	

Start early. The primary intent of adding this superhabit into the 'being effective early stage' is so that you think about what you are prepared to do over the term, semester or year (the price you are prepared to pay). For example, are you prepared to spend an hour every four weeks revising each subject? If you are, the research suggests it will have a benefit.

There is a secondary suggestion, too. As you buy your textbooks and access online resources, another way of getting ahead before the semester starts would be to skim through the topics to come. Looking at the chapter headings, the order of content and ideas that are familiar to you is a great way to go into the first class with some understanding of what is ahead. Spending 10 to 30 minutes for each subject will have you walking into that first class with a greater understanding of what is to come.

The takeaway message

Starting early shows that you are prepared to put in the work to be better than average. It puts you a step ahead of the vast majority who won't make the same effort. It allows you to preview material to make you more prepared for what happens during class time.

Will you make being effective early one of your study habits?

CHAPTER 2

Stage 2: Making term time count

"The best preparation for tomorrow is doing your best today"

H Jackson Brown Jr (American author)

Stage 1:	Stage 2:	Stage 3:	Stage 4:	Stage 5:	Stage 6:
Before the first class	Classes are on (supported by study)	SWOTVAC and exam block	24 hours before an exam	An exam routine	Feedback and reflection

The key aims of making term time count

The main aim of this period of learning is simple – you are building your foundation. When you are in class you are in the most resource-rich environment – you have a teacher, peers, your textbook, the opportunity to ask questions for clarification and, more than likely, technology to support your learning. Not only that, but once you are in the classroom, the distractions are fewer – no TV, no bed to nap on, hopefully no social media to distract you...

However, we are not just talking classes, we are also talking about the work, the study, that is done outside of class time – the summarising, revision and practising of skills. That is why study skills like using practice tests/questions, flashcards and the Pomodoro Technique are introduced here. The time when classes are on is usually the longest stage of learning – a term or a semester – and includes both time in class and time spent studying.

The period of the term, semester or year when classes are on is the ideal time to be getting the most out of class (you are there anyway, so you may as well do your best), and to do enough study so that, come the time to start preparing for an exam, you are already in great shape. Not only that, because this is usually the longest period of the learning cycle, being an effective learner during class time, and studying outside class time, positions you for success.

Study superhabits for you to use

This stage of making term time count discusses these superhabits:

Superhabit of an A+ effort in class
Superhabit of sleep
Superhabit of practice tests/questions

There are also four study strategies and tools that will help you make the most of your study time during this period of learning when you are attending classes (i.e. during a term). They are easy to implement and once you put them into practice, they support great study. They include:

Flashcards
Pomodoro Technique
Handwriting notes
Graphic organisers

Superhabit of an A+ effort in class

In order to describe how the superhabit of an A+ effort can help in making term time count, I want to start with the story of a scientist who won the Nobel Prize in Physics, Dr Isidor Rabi. He credited his intellectual success, in part, to the question his mother asked him each day when he returned from school: "Did you ask a good question today?" (Sheff, 1988).

I think it is a great link to be thinking about the habits we can use to move from just being 'compliant' during term time to moving toward what I call 'academic intensity'. Being compliant, or what we might call 'academic compliance', relates to the state many people are in during a class or lecture. They are in class and they are largely doing what is asked: they are doing some learning. However, it is all a little mediocre.

The preferred state is 'academic intensity', where a student is actively engaged with the intent of getting the most out of class. The table opposite sets out some differences between academic compliance and academic intensity; clearly, academic intensity will have the biggest learning impact.

Academic compliance	Academic intensity
Sitting with people on the basis of friendships	Being prepared to sit where the learning will be best
When the teacher/lecturer leaves the room, it is an opportunity for a social chat	When the teacher/lecturer leaves the room, it is an opportunity to keep working related to the learning
When asked to do a task in a class/tutorial, it is done to a reasonable standard	When asked to do a task in class, the student challenges themselves to work at a high level
When a question is asked by another student in class, it is a time when attention is not as important	When a question is asked by another student, it is a great opportunity to listen, answer it in your own mind and listen to the teacher/lecturer's explanation
When uncertain about some of the content, being prepared to leave it till later to look up – perhaps in the textbook (although, in reality, probably forgetting about it…)	When uncertain about some of the content, asking a question about it at the next opportunity
Notes will be a directly typed copy of the teacher/lecturer's PowerPoint or, even better, if the PowerPoint is available online notes will be cut and pasted from there	Notes are carefully written or typed, transforming them into the way they best make sense; any points of emphasis, or links with other ideas, are noted

Choosing the level of effort you are prepared to make during a class will have a significant impact on your learning.

Learning from students

In a secondary school survey of students who had the biggest increase in GPA from Semester 1 to Semester 2, it was interesting to note that one of the most common strategies behind these students' success was 'working harder during class time', with 62.2% of the improving students nominating that this was part of their success.

Superhabit of sleep

Getting eight to 10 hours of sleep at night as often as you can is likely to improve academic performance both during class time and while studying.

I live in Queensland, where we have a road campaign around the 'fatal five' things that lead to crashes. Two of the fatal five relate to superhabits of study: fatigue (superhabit of sleep) and distraction (superhabit of single-tasking). Many of the concepts that we talk about in this book are not just about study – you can take them into other environments. Getting enough sleep and working without distractions are important to both good study and safe driving.

Heather Turgeon and Julie Wright's (2022) book *Generation Sleepless* is about young adults not getting enough sleep, the negative impacts of not getting enough sleep and what can be done to improve sleep. Key messages from their book include:

- The habit of quality sleep can improve mental health, improve academic grades, reduce stress and anxiety, and improve health.
- Fewer than half the young adults of high school age through to their early 20s are getting enough sleep.
- Nine to 10 hours of sleep per night for a teen is optimal, with eight to eight and a half hours adequate.
- Having time away from technology in the 30 minutes that you wind down to sleep helps improve sleep quality.

Generation Sleepless includes great ideas on establishing night-time and morning routines, and on improving sleep quality. If you feel you are not regularly getting at least eight hours per night, are struggling to fall asleep or quality sleep continues to be a challenge, look for more support, perhaps from a doctor or other expert.

Learning from students

Psychology students in a school in my area carried out some interesting research. For three nights a group of 46 students recorded their normal sleep with electronic devices in their bedroom. Then, for another three nights, the same students recorded their sleep without electronic devices in their bedroom. They found that average sleep time improved from 7 hours and 56 minutes to 8 hours and 15 minutes.

Is removing technology from the bedroom a price that you are prepared to pay for better sleep, and the benefits that better sleep brings?

Superhabit of practice tests/questions

There is a very interesting research article relating to the superhabit of practice tests/questions. John Dunlosky from Kent State University and a group of researchers set out to compare 10 common learning techniques, from rereading the textbook to using practice tests/questions for self-testing. They split the 10 techniques into those that had 'low utility' (low usefulness), those that had 'moderate utility' (some usefulness) and those that had 'high utility' (most useful) (Dunlosky et al. 2013).

The 'low utility' study habits included rereading, highlighting and summarising. These are three very common study habits, which the researchers found only had low usefulness.

They found two 'high utility' study habits: 1) the superhabit of starting early, or 'distributed practice', which we looked at in Stage 1 – it means regularly revising material over time, rather than cramming; and 2) 'practice testing', which Dunlosky et al. (2013) define as "self-testing or taking practice tests over to-be-learned materials". The authors of the research make it clear that 'practice testing' includes testing that students are able to undertake on their own, including writing and using flashcards, as well as questions that might be provided through end-of-chapter questions or textbook exercises.

The core of using the superhabit of practice tests/questions is that you are finding or writing yourself questions that you then try to answer before checking any answers. This provides three important benefits:

1. Retrieving information from your memory is a great way of revising it (the research phrase for this is 'retrieval practice').

2. Using practice questions gives you great information about what you do know and what you don't yet know (so long as you don't cheat and read the answer before you answer the practice question).

3. Answering practice questions allows you to practise what you have to do in the exam.

Practice tests/questions can be used to make study efforts more effective during this stage of learning during term time.

Flashcards

The use of flashcards is closely related to the superhabit of practice tests/questions. Dunlosky et al. (2013) identify the use of 'practice testing' as a 'high utility' strategy, and their article mentions flashcards as a strategy six times, so we can deduce that it is a simple and effective way to study.

To see this study strategy in practice, let's assume a Legal Studies student has to learn the Queensland court hierarchy. They might write this question on one side of a piece of paper: *List the courts in the Queensland court hierarchy*. On the other side of the paper they might write the answer: *Magistrates Court, District Court, Supreme Court, the Queensland Civil and Administrative Tribunal hearing minor civil disputes and the High Court of Australia hearing appeals*. When the student comes to test themselves, they read the question, jot down an answer and then compare their answer with the one on the flashcard. Over the course of a term, semester or year, they can build up a set of flashcards, allowing them increasingly thorough practice tests on the content.

As a quick aside, it is important to take the time to answer the question without looking at the answer on the flashcard. Ensure that you are retrieving the information, not just turning the flashcard over and assuming that because the information looks familiar, you have got it.

Pomodoro Technique

The Pomodoro Technique is named after the tomato-shaped kitchen timer that was first used with the technique.

This technique is a simple one and goes like this:

- You do 15 to 25 minutes of study
- Then take a five-minute break
- Then do another 15 to 25 minutes of study
- Take another five-minute break
- Repeat for three or four study blocks, then have a longer break – perhaps 30 minutes

Along with this, you:

- Set a clear goal at the start of each block of time (for example, 'I want to work on Chapter 2 maths questions').
- Set aside all distractions (social media, mobile phone) when you are studying (so important!).

And there you have it, the Pomodoro Technique and a simple recipe for intentional study for a realistic amount of time in a low-distraction environment.

There are two TED talks from young students who reflect positively on the impact the Pomodoro Technique has had on their learning. In a 2019 TEDx talk, Yana Savitsky described the way the Pomodoro Technique "has the power to change your life", with short blocks of study allowing you to "set aside the constant distractions" that hamper effective learning. Arib Malik, in a 2023 TEDxYouth talk, discussed the way "distractions" and "the cacophony of sounds of notifications on my phone" had made study ineffective. However, using the Pomodoro Technique had helped him stay focused and motivated, and avoid the "mental fatigue of long blocks of study".

Handwriting notes

Writing in *The Economist* magazine (2023), the columnist Johnson looked at some of the research suggesting benefits of taking handwritten notes as a student, rather than typing up notes. A key study that was referred to showed that when students typed notes they wrote more words, but almost exactly the same words that had been presented on the board/data projector. While typing, students were not processing the information into their own words. On the other hand, students who handwrote notes had fewer words, but had translated the presented notes into their own words.

It is easier to add to handwritten notes, for example, underlining something for emphasis or drawing a quick line to acknowledge a connection. If you prefer typing up notes, try to move away from typing them exactly as they appear, and instead translate them into your own understanding. Remember to highlight important elements and find connections. Doing this is a great way of making the most of class time.

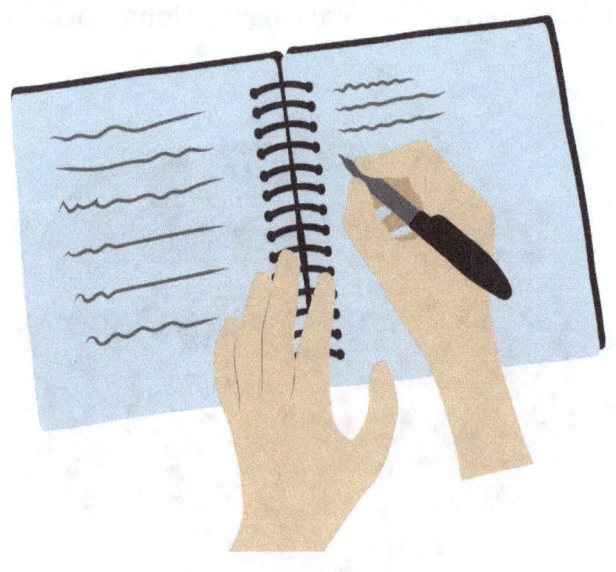

Graphic organisers

Displaying information in a graphical form, most commonly on a flowchart or mind map, might make it easier for you to see hierarchies in the information; information closest to the centre tends to be more important. It is sometimes clearer to see connections on a graphic because the information is on just one page with an image, making it easier to remember compared to a block of text.

Marzano et al. (2001) identified the use of graphic organisers as one of nine strategies that led to improved student achievement, associating them with a 27% improvement in learning.

Here is a graphic showing how mind maps can work:

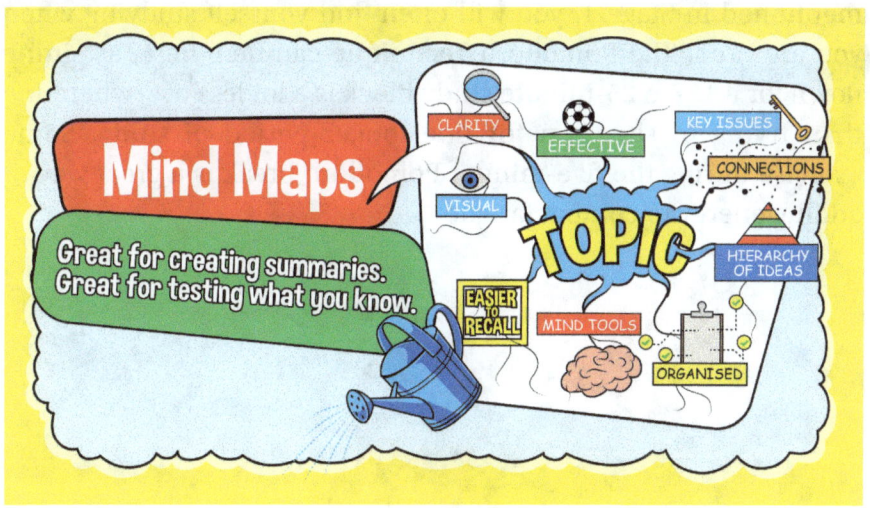

Putting things into practice

When you are in the classroom, lecture theatre or tutorial room, you have a choice: work at a level of 'academic compliance' or at a level of 'academic intensity' – what is the price you are prepared to pay? Having made the effort to show up, you may as well make the most of that time and build a strong foundation for your learning.

A simple first step, as we have looked at, is how you will choose to take notes – mindlessly typing using a laptop, or being more deliberate, even writing notes by hand.

Your term, semester and year are busy times, and despite setting up a workable weekly planner at the start of the semester, as mentioned in Stage 1, you will often find yourself studying when you are tired. The Pomodoro Technique can help here, as sitting down for a 15- to 25-minute study block is a lot less overwhelming than trying to sit down for one longer period of study. Some exercise during the five-minute Pomodoro break is a great way of adding energy to combat fatigue.

Over the weeks in class, there are two 'cumulative' study tasks you can work on: building a set of flashcards and creating graphic organisers (such as a mind map or flowchart) that summarises the content. You can do the latter on an A3 or even A2 page. The flashcards become useful revision tools if, every week or two, you update the set by adding new questions. Similarly, adding the content learned from the past week or two gives you an increasingly up-to-date flowchart that provides a 'one-stop' visual summary of what you have learned. It can also become a 'practice test' tool where you set yourself the 'practice question' challenge of drawing the flowchart from scratch. It will quickly give you some positive feedback about what you know, and what you need to learn in more depth.

Building and using flashcards and testing your ability to recreate a mind map become effective ways of incorporating the superhabit of practice tests/questions into your study.

All this is supported by, as often as possible, getting the eight to 10 hours of sleep that you need to perform at your best, helping memory, recall and enhancing mood. This helps in all areas of life, not just study. For example, NBA great LeBron James has often talked about the important role sleep plays in his pursuit of elite performance. Sekaran (2023) talks about the fact that LeBron James is highly focused on getting eight or nine hours of sleep per night, and sometimes even 10, to help support his best performance.

The takeaway message

The term time phase of your learning usually takes up the longest period of time. It is the environment with the most resources: peers, teacher, textbook, online resources. The opportunity is there for you to use this time to build the foundation for your learning in the classroom.

Over this period, there is also the opportunity to go beyond the 'low utility' study skills of highlighting, summarising and rereading. Setting time aside to work deliberately using the Pomodoro Technique and 'high utility' strategies like flashcards gives you the strategies to continue the foundation you started with a deliberate effort during term time. These strategies add intensity to your work. This links to two key ideas that were introduced at the start of the book:

1. Study impact = intensity of effort × time
2. Perhaps most important of all, if you are sitting down to study, do it well; after all, life is too good for bad study

CHAPTER 3

Stage 3: Taking advantage of SWOTVAC and exam block

"Before anything else, preparation is the key to success"

Alexander Graham Bell

Stage 1:	Stage 2:	Stage 3:	Stage 4:	Stage 5:	Stage 6:
Before the first class	Classes are on (supported by study)	SWOTVAC and exam block	24 hours before an exam	An exam routine	Feedback and reflection

The key aims of taking advantage of SWOTVAC and exam block

Some students are fortunate to have a block of time in which to put together specific preparation for exams. This is called SWOTVAC ('study without teaching vacation') and exam block, and can be a week or two in which students can find extra time and energy to lift their subject knowledge and skills to a higher level. The key aim of this chapter is to think about how you best take advantage of this time – consistent with the best understanding of how effective study works.

If things have gone smoothly in a subject up to the start of SWOTVAC, you should have a solid understanding of the subject built on effective involvement in class, starting early on revision activities, and the use of effective learning aids like flashcards and mind maps.

A SWOTVAC and exam block period enables you to enjoy some quality study when there is less on, for example, no classes. In addition, you also might reduce the number of shifts at work and choose to have less social engagement during this time. Taking advantage of this extra time and using your energy for study is the key aim of the SWOTVAC and exam block time.

Study superhabits for you to use

We will discuss these two study superhabits in this chapter:

Superhabit of single-tasking
Superhabit of a deliberate mindset

We will also look at:

Understanding flow

Superhabit of single-tasking

Even though it is being introduced at the SWOTVAC and exam block stage, the superhabit of single-tasking (focusing on doing just one thing) is important throughout all learning and studying activities.

The following quote is a succinct summary of the peril of multi-tasking:

> "To do two things at the same time
> is to do neither"
>
> **Publilius Syrus (Latin writer)**

Single-tasking is the opposite of multi-tasking: single-tasking is a focus on one activity at a time, whereas multi-tasking is where we try to juggle more than one thing at once. For a study session, multi-tasking might include a TV on in the background, reading messages from social media while also having email open – all at the same time as trying to study.

Research shows that multi-tasking can significantly reduce learning and increase feelings of stress.

As an example of how multi-tasking hurts productivity, conduct this mini experiment (without writing anything down).

There are 12 letters in the word 'multi-tasking'. Time yourself on how long it takes you to spell multi-tasking and then count to 12. So, you will go: 'M U L T I T A S K I N G, then 1, 2, 3, 4… up to 12. This tends to take five to six seconds for the average person.

Now do it alternating between letters and numbers. So, you will go: M 1 U 2 L 3 T 4…

Multi-tasking in this way of combining spelling and counting often takes the average person 12 to 15 seconds.

This example shows how multi-tasking reduces performance.

Another practical example of multi-tasking reducing performance is relayed in an article by Annie Murphy Paul (2013) in the California State University Learning Center. In the article Paul describes a study by Dr Larry Rosen, a professor and author with a particular interest in the impact of distractions on learning. Dr Rosen and his investigators observed students who had been given time to study 'something important'. They watched what the students did. After only two minutes, some students started to check social media or respond to text messages. Over a period of 15 minutes, students were distracted more than a third of the time, even though they had the opportunity to complete some study.

"We were amazed at how frequently they multi-tasked, even though they knew someone was watching," Dr Rosen said. "It really seems that they could not go for 15 minutes without engaging their devices. Young people have a wildly inflated idea of how many things they can attend to at once."

Paul's (2013) article considers the negative impact of multi-tasking, finding "evidence from psychology, cognitive science and neuroscience suggests that when students multi-task while doing schoolwork, their learning is far spottier and shallower than if the work had their full attention. They understand and remember less".

Given that understanding and remembering are crucial to learning, the negative impacts of multi-tasking while studying are, hopefully, relatively clear.

Superhabit of a deliberate mindset

The core of this superhabit is that you have some control over your thought process in different situations. For example, you are sitting down for an exam. As you read the questions, you realise that the exam will be challenging – more difficult than you anticipated. Your initial reaction is likely to be some unhappiness, a little fear, concern or nervousness. You might initially think the exam is too hard and that you're not going to do well. However, you *do* have some control over your thoughts.

You are likely to be in a large hall full of other students who are doing the same exam as you – and there's a good chance that some of them are also finding the exam challenging. Therefore, you might change your thinking to, 'the exam is tough for everyone; if I can stay calm and work hard, I am sure that I can do as well as anyone'.

As a teacher who prepares Year 12 students for end-of-year external exams, one focus I have with them is preparing for what to do if the exam they are sitting is particularly challenging. I try to get them to see this as a potential advantage – if they can stay calm, work hard and think carefully about the best approach to each question, chances are they will be ahead of many of the students who become rattled by a tough exam.

'Mindset' can be defined as the 'set of attitudes held by someone'. For the purpose of this discussion, I think a better definition might be the 'set of attitudes held by someone, and the understanding that these attitudes can be deliberate'. That is, you can influence your mindset, and therefore, influence your reaction to a situation.

I want to introduce three mindset ideas that you can use to encourage an effective work ethic during exam block, or at any stage of the learning process:

- **Grit** – the ability to work with effort and passion toward long-term goals
- **Growth mindset** – the value of persisting when work is challenging, or where you have initially failed, because that is what builds capacity
- **Hard choices** – where you get to decide 'who am I to be?' when you have to choose between two activities, for example, going to the movies (fun and social) or getting some study done (improving academically)

Grit is an idea discussed in Professor Angela Duckworth's 2013 TED talk *Grit: The Power of Passion and Perseverance*. Her introduction to the idea of grit came through her observations of students while she was teaching – what made students successful? Indeed, she considered what made people in a variety of situations successful, from spelling bees to the military.

Her research identified 'grit' as being important to success, which she defined as:

> "Grit is passion and perseverance for very long-term goals. Grit is having stamina. Grit is sticking with your future, day in, day out, not just for the week, not just for the month, but for years, and working really hard to make that future a reality. Grit is living life like it's a marathon, not a sprint."

Being aware of grit, challenging yourself as to what it means for you, having a clear long-term goal in mind and being passionate about your future will support your study efforts. Watch Professor Duckworth's TED talk about grit to find out more.

Professor Carol Dweck talks about **growth mindset** in the 2014 TED talk *The Power of Believing that you can Improve*.

The core idea behind a growth mindset is that challenging work and mistakes (that we learn from) are what increases our capacity. Those learners that 'lean into' a challenge, knowing that they are going to learn from the challenge if they choose to persist rather than give up, do better than those who shy away from a challenge.

A growth mindset helps us when we are confronted by challenging work, for example, a difficult maths concept. The mindset that we *are* capable of learning the work even if we don't 'get it' initially, and sticking with the work, will build our capacity, help us to persist, try different ways, seek help from different sources and, finally, make progress.

The opposite is a 'fixed mindset', which downplays the possibility of growth. In the example of a difficult maths concept, a student with a fixed mindset is more likely to say, "I am just not a maths person", and give up on the task sooner.

Professor Dweck has studied people across many different activities and found that a growth mindset is important to success across different endeavours. Her TED talk and her book are great sources of further information.

Professor Ruth Chang defines the mindset idea of **hard choices** in this way:

> "In a hard choice, one alternative is better in some ways, the other alternative is better in other ways, and neither is better than the other overall."

An example of a hard choice might be deciding whether to go to the movies on a Sunday afternoon (which will be social and enjoyable) or staying home and studying (which supports your goal to be a successful student). Professor Chang says that when there is no clearly better option, we have the opportunity to make an important choice around who we are to be. In her words:

> "When we choose between options that are on a par, we can do something really rather remarkable. We can put our very selves behind an option. Here's where I stand. Here's who I am.
>
> "So, when we face hard choices, we shouldn't beat our head against a wall trying to figure out which alternative is better. There is no best alternative. Instead of looking for reasons out there, we should be looking for reasons in here: Who am I to be?"

So, back to the hard choice of going to a movie or studying. Early in the term, when the workload is well under control, the 'who am I to be?' answer might be the person who goes to the movies. Later in the term, as exams are nearer, the 'who am I to be?' answer might be the student working to improve themselves.

Professor Chang's 2014 TED talk *How to Make Hard Choices* provides a great framework for turning 'hard choices' into decisions about 'who am I to be?'.

Understanding flow

Flow, or 'being in the zone', is something that we might associate with athletes or performers who describe 'flow/being in the zone' as times of high-level achievement/performance coming with little effort. Dr Gareth Furber, in the 2022 article 'Achieving the Psychological State of Flow' for the Flinders University website, described flow (or being in the zone) in the following way:

> "When someone is in flow, they are intensely focused and concentrated on the task at hand, they become less self-conscious, they feel more in control, they tend to lose time. It is a state of total immersion where the border between the task and one's awareness disappears.
>
> "It is a desirable state for a number of reasons. It is associated with increases in happiness, creativity, productivity, and means a person is more likely to re-engage with the activity in the future."

One of the benefits of a SWOTVAC and exam block period is that you have longer periods of time to study – you are not cramming your study into evenings after school or university, so perhaps you are a little less tired when you study. This provides a unique opportunity to try and be deliberate about how you organise your study, in the hope that it is increasingly productive, and perhaps even more enjoyable. I am unsure as to how often students enter a flow state when they study, however, adopting the ideas that lead to a flow state will lead to more effective study sessions.

Dr Furber's article contains the following ideas for students looking to move into a state of flow as they study (you may recognise some of our superhabits of study in this list):

- Be specific about the task you are going to do, for example, 'write down the 10 most important facts from chapter 10'. You might notice that this is similar to having a clear objective at the start of each Pomodoro session.

- Break down tasks into achievable chunks. The example Dr Furber provides is creating flashcards one chapter at a time for an exam.

- Ensure there is feedback. Dr Furber gives examples of feedback as ticking items off a to-do list as they are complete or checking progress through self-testing.

- Work at your best times. If you are more alert in the morning, use that time. If you are more alert in the afternoon, that is the time for you. However, wasting the day playing computer games or scrolling social media and then trying to study in the evening when you are tired is clearly not a great strategy.

- Remove distractions (including digital distractions).

- Try and elicit a positive mood going into tasks. Dr Furber suggests activities like a cup of tea or coffee, meditation, a little time in nature or some physical exercise like a walk are ways to move into study feeling positive.

- Push through the struggle phase. Dr Furber warns that the first 15 to 20 minutes of focused work can be challenging, but this is a natural part of moving into our work.

- Emphasise learning over task achievement. Dr Furber encourages us to look beyond just the task (for example, 'create flashcards for chapter 11 of the Legal Studies text'), to acknowledge that, as we study, we are building important skills and knowledge. If we can frame a task such as 'create flashcards for chapter 11 of the Legal Studies text so we build our knowledge of the tort of defamation,' we can link to the bigger picture that through study we are building important knowledge and skills.

- Set a timer. Similar to the Pomodoro Technique, Dr Furber emphasises that it is related to single-tasking. He suggests longer work periods of 40 minutes or more, and encourages us to experiment. During the SWOTVAC and exam block time, you should be less fatigued, and therefore capable of longer study sessions. Ultimately, though, you want to find what works best for you.

Ransom Patterson (2018) wrote an article for College Info Geek: 'The Flow State: How to Enter Your Brain's Most Productive State'. In his article he considered 'how to achieve flow', and came up with the following suggestions:

- Make sure you aren't hungry.

- Cut out distractions, with ideas including wearing headphones, shutting the door or using the Pomodoro Technique.

- Use the Pomodoro Technique, with suggestions that this is a great way to help you get started, which Patterson describes as the biggest mental barrier.

- Don't multitask. Patterson reminds us that every time we switch from one task to another, it takes time for the brain to adjust to the new task.

- Get enough high-quality sleep.

Putting things into practice

Since most students seem to have a week or two of SWOTVAC and exam block and then exams spread over time, the first practical step to highlight is that of getting started early, a superhabit we first looked at in Stage 1. A motivated student will, by this stage of a subject, already use several experiences of 'spaced practice', to revise material over time. And, by working efficiently at the very beginning of a SWOTVAC and exam block, there is a chance to have further 'spaced practice' review periods before the exam.

This desire to take advantage of the start of SWOTVAC and exam block for learning matches well with the superhabit of using a weekly planner, also first looked at in Stage 1, although with SWOTVAC and exam block, you need to see how much time is available without class commitments, and start to schedule study sessions for the time of day you work best. Remember to include some fun activities, especially if SWOTVAC and exam block runs for multiple weeks. One difference with a SWOTVAC and exam block study plan compared to your usual weekly planner is that you are unlikely to follow the same schedule of subject each week; you'll need to plan for some extra study times early for subjects with higher weighting or importance, or exams that are scheduled earlier.

As you think about your schedule over SWOTVAC and exam block, be sure to get eight to 10 hours of sleep each night for a great foundation for effective study. There is never a bad time to reiterate the importance of sleep to support study and learning – see Stage 2 for more details on this.

Your study location is one aspect you have some flexibility over. You could try studying in a variety of different settings, for example, splitting study times between the school/university library, the local library, outdoors in a park if the weather is right, and at home. Having multiple study environments could be effective as they provide different location cues that might help you to recall information. Some students identify that studying in the vicinity of motivated peers acts as a 'positive contagion' that helps with their own motivation. However you choose your study location, the flexibility that you have during SWOTVAC and exam block means you can be deliberate about this choice.

> ### Learning from students
>
> As a high school teacher, I run a number of study sessions (after school and on Saturday mornings) where students can attend and work alongside other peers who are studying. One year I did a survey of the students who attended the sessions most often and 96.2% 'agreed' or 'strongly agreed' that they found working alongside other students to be a positive motivator.
>
> Some comments from the students included:
>
> "A quiet place with other people studying helps my motivation."
>
> "I appreciate the work ethic of those people around me."
>
> "The study sessions offer a space for all people who take their studies seriously to join together in a distraction-free environment to complete their work."

Moving on to 'how' to study, I suggest you keep these three study ideas – which have been introduced in more detail in Stage 2 – in mind as you get started during your SWOTVAC and exam block:

1. Mind maps
2. Practice tests/questions (and flashcards)
3. The Pomodoro Technique

If you have been on top of your study leading into SWOTVAC and exam block, you may already have mind maps/flashcards prepared for each subject. If not, it is a good idea to start this now: create mind maps to summarise and set out the key information for each subject, and flashcards to build a set of practice questions that you can use for self-testing.

Mind maps can be a great self-testing tool: setting up a timed challenge to create a mind map of all the content you can remember gives an insight into what you know well and what content you will benefit from revising further. Creating a mind map from memory is an example of 'retrieval practice', fitting into the superhabit of practice tests/questions, and is an effective strategy for increasing the ability to recall information.

SWOTVAC and exam block is a time when you may have access to further practice test/question resources. This could include resources provided by your teacher/lecturer and past exam papers – on top of resources like end-of-chapter questions, and questions you have identified yourself. Using these early, so they provide feedback on where you are up to, is a positive application of the superhabits of practice tests/questions and starting early (spaced practice), as you still have time to learn from the practice exam.

The Pomodoro Technique is a great way to get started on each study session: set out the key objective of a 15- to 25-minute study session, remove distractions and get to work – knowing that there is a break at the end.

Keep in mind the earlier discussion on flow as you think about the practicality of studying during the SWOTVAC and exam block time. The fundamentals of being well rested, having a clear objective in mind, breaking tasks down into smaller elements and then ticking them off your to-do list as they are completed, and managing distractions remain important. The more aspirational elements, including recognising the learning elements of a task (not just 'summarising Chapter 10', but understanding the importance of the content behind it, i.e. 'summarising Chapter 10 to better understand the way culture impacts organisations') and adopting habits that can increase mood (short walks, a cup of tea or coffee) have value.

The role of exercise during study breaks

I want to throw in an extra practical idea at this point – that a walk (or a jog or other form of exercise) might be the ultimate study break. Fenesi et al. (2018) considered the role of exercise for students in research published in the *Journal of Applied Research in Memory and Cognition*. The study considered the impact of five-minute exercise breaks on students attending a lecture. The authors summarised their findings as:

> "Exercise breaks promoted attention throughout the lecture compared to no breaks and non-exercise breaks, and resulted in superior learning when assessed on immediate and delayed tests."

David DiSalvo, author of *What Makes your Brain Happy and Why You Should do the Opposite*, writing in *Forbes* (2018), considered the importance of exercise as having a positive impact on the brain. He wrote:

> "We know from previous research that walking is a remarkable brain booster – even short bursts of walking produce meaningful results.

> "The research also tangentially supports the idea of exercising at lunch. The benefits of increased blood flow for the brain are well-evidenced, even after just a few minutes of cardio. A mid-day burst could help move the cognitive wheels through the afternoon.

> "You can insert your light exercise of choice, walking or otherwise – the point remains that weaving movement into your day can help your brain manage information and sharpen your attention. That's an edge most of us could use, especially since the challenge to stay focused amidst endless distractions is only getting more intense."

Given other research around the immediate impacts of exercise that include enhanced mood and alertness, the benefit of increased attention and superior learning identified in this research, that looked at a cohort of students, provides more evidence that using exercise as part of your study breaks is a strategy worth considering.

The takeaway message

SWOTVAC and exam block is an exciting opportunity that gives you more time to focus on your study in the lead-up to exams. Taking advantage of this, in a deliberate way, puts you in a great position to perform well on exam day.

Here are some final comments on the SWOTVAC and exam block period:

When and where? Build a planner for the SWOTVAC and exam block time, and consider how you might use different locations to build variety while enjoying the positive influence of others as you study. Longer periods of the day available for study means more opportunity to schedule study when it suits you, and less studying when you are tired at night. This is also a great opportunity to get eight to 10 hours of sleep to be at your best when you perform academically at a high level.

How? The fundamentals of good study don't change. Working without distractions, using the Pomodoro Technique, practice tests/questions, flashcards and other practice materials (including past exam papers and revision questions from your teacher/lecturer) are good strategies to use, while mind maps are useful to see what you know. Setting up and ticking off to-do lists and building a planner of study times remain great organisational tools.

Other study ideas. The idea of 'flow' during study enables you to manage your study and help you work better, from starting with a mood-enhancing activity like a coffee and removing distractions through to working with an objective in mind, while being deliberate with your study breaks. A little exercise to boost alertness and attention can also have a positive impact.

CHAPTER 4

Stage 4: The 24 hours before an exam

"Finishing strong is a powerful demonstration of commitment, character, integrity and heart"

Gary Ryan Blair (author)

Stage 1: Before the first class	Stage 2: Classes are on (supported by study)	Stage 3: SWOTVAC and exam block	Stage 4: 24 hours before an exam	Stage 5: An exam routine	Stage 6: Feedback and reflection

The key aims of the 24 hours before an exam

Basketball is my sport, and I have been lucky to know people involved in basketball in Australia at a professional level and had the chance, on occasion, to watch how professional basketballers go about their business.

I can see significant similarities in how a professional basketballer/basketball team approaches the 24 hours before a game and how a student might approach their last 24 hours before an exam.

For a basketballer, the focus is on key elements, including:

- Travelling (if needed), being well rested and in good physical shape for the game
- Having a final review of individual and team responsibilities for the game – the knowledge needed for the game
- Having a 'shoot around' on the day of the game, including a chance to focus on individual skills
- Making sure everyone is organised for the game, from strapping ankles to ensuring team uniforms are ready

For a student approaching an exam, these ideas work well to provide a framework for what can be achieved in the 24 hours prior to an exam:

- Making sure you are well rested and ready to perform at your best
- Having some time to review the knowledge and skills you need for the exam
- Being well organised for the exam

Study superhabits for you to use

Three study superhabits for you to focus on in the 24 hours leading up to an exam include:

Superhabit of sleep
Superhabit of starting early (or 'spaced practice')
Superhabit of single-tasking

Superhabit of sleep

Understanding the importance of sleep to quality performance this far into the book should be a given. If you can get your eight to 10 hours of sleep leading up to the exam, and in the days prior, then you are in great shape to perform at your best on the day.

Superhabit of starting early

The superhabit of starting early, or spaced practice, has been an important one, even from before the first class. Students who don't respect the value of starting early or using spaced practice will be 'cramming' study during the 24 hours before an exam.

The theory behind starting early/spaced practice still has value for well-prepared students who don't need to cram. An important researcher, Ebbinghaus, found that the more frequently you are exposed to material, the better you remember it, and with each revision, you forget it more slowly. That makes the last 24 hours before an exam a great time to revise; using an effective study strategy like flashcards to answer practice questions can be an ideal way to have a last, thorough, revision of the content.

Superhabit of single-tasking

Single-tasking is closely linked to your organisation in the 24 hours before the exam. If you are well prepared for your exam – arriving early with equipment organised and important details like your student ID card with you – your focus can be on the exam. Being organised so that you are not wasting energy, effort or stress with distractions like rushing to find a park or your student ID card is the ideal scenario.

Putting things into practice

On a practical level, if you have been influenced by what you've read so far in this book, you will come into the last 24 hours before an exam with a different challenge to those who have crammed (they are in for a stressful final 24 hours!).

You will appreciate the value of sleep to quality performance and will be in a position to get as good a night's sleep as you can.

You can use the 24 hours before an exam to improve your ability to recall material by re-testing yourself, and then focus on deepening your knowledge of any material that you are unsure of, without relying on these final 24 hours to cram the bulk of your revision.

If you have made flashcards of practice questions, they are an ideal tool to be using now. Another approach is to test yourself by seeing how effectively you can create, from memory, a mind map of the topics in the exam. Both of these methods are examples of 'retrieval practice', providing an effective way to put the finishing touches on your study.

Being well prepared for the exam avoids unnecessary stress. Knowing that you are well organised and have all the equipment you need – like pencils for multiple-choice responses or downloaded software on a laptop – allows your focus to only be on the exam.

The takeaway message

Assuming you come into the final 24 hours before an exam well prepared, having done a recent and thorough revision of material, without the stress of last-minute cramming, you will be able to sit the exam in a well-rested, well-organised state.

CHAPTER 5

Stage 5: Building an exam routine

"Being your best when your best is needed. The ability to enjoy challenges when things become difficult and to derive exhilaration from them"

John Wooden (basketball coach and teacher)

Stage 1: Before the first class	Stage 2: Classes are on (supported by study)	Stage 3: SWOTVAC and exam block	Stage 4: 24 hours before an exam	Stage 5: An exam routine	Stage 6: Feedback and reflection

The key aims of building an exam routine

As I write this, NBA great LeBron James is 39 years old and still playing basketball at a high level in the NBA. When it comes to the habits behind his greatness, much is written about his focus on getting great sleep, eating right and training hard. One habit that is not talked about as much is his pre-game routine. Joshua Rogers (2023), writing for talkSPORT, outlined the way James arrives four hours before tip-off to go through a pre-game routine that includes cardio to warm up, shooting and dribbling skills, and a pre-game warm-up with his team: a four-hour routine to help him perform at his best.

Building an exam routine has the same aim – providing a routine that helps you perform at your best when it counts, during the exam.

Study superhabits for you to use

The superhabits of study that are applied in this stage will focus on:

Superhabit of setting goals (to focus performance)
Superhabit of a deliberate mindset

Other study strategies include:

Routines
Exercise

Superhabit of setting goals

A 2017 article on the Premier Sport Psychology website divides possible goals into three types:

- Outcome goals (similar to what you might have set at the start of the subject, an open or SMART goal)
- Performance goals
- Process goals (these look at the behaviours that are in our control, things that put us in a good position to achieve our outcome goals)

I suggest that, for the exam, you focus on process goals.

Using a sports perspective, Premier Sport Psychology identified process goals as being activities such as drinking enough water, working out regularly and journaling for feedback.

Setting a process goal prior to an exam is useful to remind you of the elements that you can control during an exam, including tasks such as using planning time well, reading questions carefully, managing time, and being aware of effort and attention over the exam time. One positive thing about having a process goal is that it moves the focus away from any concern about how much you know toward what you are going to do during the exam.

Superhabit of a deliberate mindset

The superhabit of a deliberate mindset can be applied to the exam situation. There will be challenges throughout an exam that you can't control. Keep in mind the idea of grit (perseverance toward goals when there is challenge), a growth mindset (it is the challenging work that builds growth – even during an exam) and your ability to be deliberate in choosing your response to the challenges of exams, and you will be able to work toward putting your best responses on paper (or online) during the exam.

If, as part of your exam routine, you remind yourself that you can be deliberate about your reaction to exam situations, and take time to choose a productive reaction, you give yourself an important advantage.

Routines

One key point of having an exam routine is that the brain seems to thrive on routine. Dr Michael Nagel (Francis & Nagel, 2023) wrote:

> "Routine, routine, routine... this is not just important in terms of learning but also something the brain thrives on! One of the common challenges with exams is anxiety... One way of alleviating such anxiety is through having a planned routine and using that routine consistently."

Neuroscientist Dr Gerhard Roth (n.d.) had this to say about the brain and routine:

> "Our brains strive to turn everything into a routine because thinking is time-consuming! Routines help our brain conserve energy and minimise risks."

If a routine helps the brain thrive, reduces anxiety and conserves energy (prior to the effort of an exam), then building an exam routine has value.

Exercise

Something you might include in your exam routine is exercise. Hillman et al. (2009) considered the impact that 20 minutes of walking had on students' brains. Using imaging technology, they showed that there was significantly more brain activity after students had taken a 20-minute walk. This put those students in a great position to sit an exam because of the improved brain function.

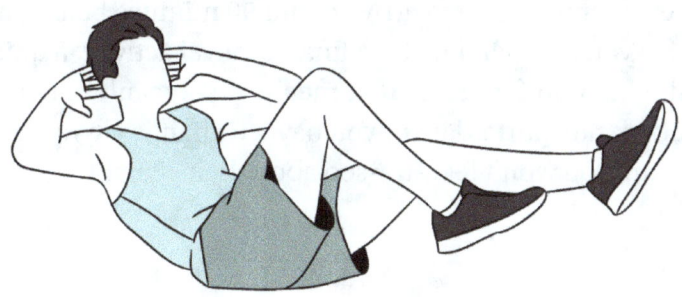

Putting things into practice

Just as LeBron James is one of the few basketball players arriving four hours before a game, your exam routine, if you choose to build one, will be based on the decisions you make about how you perform at your best.

Your answers to the following seven questions can help you start to build your own exam routine:

1. How long before the exam do you want to be in the exam area/environment?

The time of the exam itself, plus any commitments you have before the exam (for example, if you have two exams on the same day), might limit your ability to arrive early and prepare before the exam.

That said, if you have a midmorning or afternoon exam, and it is the only commitment of the day, you can decide how long before the exam you want to arrive. Things to consider might include which revision tasks you want to do before your exam and whether you want to squeeze in a 20-minute walk first.

I'd suggest that planning to arrive about 90 minutes before an exam might give you enough time for a final retrieval activity, a quick walk and still a 'margin for error'. That means if you can't find a parking spot, public transport is late or you have to change a tyre on the way to the exam, you won't feel stressed about being late.

2. What last revision/retrieval tasks do you want to complete?

My general preference when I was studying was to test myself and check that I could build a final mind map of the subject being tested. However, you might prefer to answer some revision questions with flashcards for the last time. Flashcards are particularly worth considering with Mathematics/Science/Statistics subjects, where you can practise completing the types of questions you anticipate seeing in the exam. You can 'warm up' doing a series of these questions.

3. Do you want to have time for a quick, brain-boosting walk just before the exam?

A 20-minute walk seems to increase brain activity in students, which is ideal before an exam. A walk might also help alertness if you're feeling tired. If you're feeling nervous, Marcia Purse (2024) suggests deep breathing to calm nerves; there are simple techniques called 'box/square breathing' or a 'psychological sigh' – you can find details online.

If you go for a walk, then aim to finish five to 10 minutes before the exam starts, at the exam location.

4. Do you want to set a process goal for the exam?

As a student, my thinking was that a process goal took me away from being concerned about how much I knew in the exam (there was nothing I could do about that once the exam had started), and made me think about how I wanted to behave in an exam.

An example of a process goal might be, 'I am going to work hard for the whole two hours; use my planning time to prepare my extended response; engage with the questions carefully, including underlining key words; quickly complete the questions I am comfortable with; and then spend time attempting all the remaining questions'.

5. Do you have a plan for content you are worried about?

Sometimes students will go into an exam worried about some content. If it is a Law/Legal Studies exam, they might be concerned about remembering the details of the court hierarchy.

I suggest that, as soon as you are allowed to write, you jot down as much detail of the content as you can. For example, you might be allowed to write on planning paper during planning/perusal time. Once you have written that down, you know you are part of the way to having the content you find the most challenging.

6. Do you have a strategy to manage your time?

Not managing time in exams can be disastrous. Not getting to the last 10% of questions or not finishing the last 10% of an essay might not seem a huge deal, however, it might mean that a whole marking criterion is left with no answers, bringing the overall grade down dramatically. Equally, going over word limits and having some of your writing excluded from being marked can have a significant negative influence on results.

Understanding the exam format and having a plan to distribute your time across all areas of the exam seems a simple strategy, but is worth doing to ensure the best possible grade.

7. What will you do in the challenging moments of the exam?

We talked about mindset earlier in this chapter and how it relates to the challenges in an exam. Taking some time to be ready for tricky questions and deciding how you are going to react (for example, a breathing exercise, rereading the question, carefully planning the response) puts you in a better position to deal with these inevitable moments of challenge as well as you can.

One last thought: is there a superstition that you might add to your exam routine? Lucky socks? A lucky pen? Beyond just being fun, Damisch et al. (2010) found that there might be some performance benefits for people who added a superstition to what they did, suggesting that the superstition helped give people an extra boost of confidence.

The takeaway message

Your exam routine should be exactly that: *your* routine.

Building it, reflecting on it and improving are things that you can do as part of your journey as a student during this stage of exam study.

CHAPTER 6

Stage 6: Feedback and reflection

"Self-reflection is one of the most underused yet powerful tools for success"

Richard Carlson (American author and motivational speaker)

Stage 1: Before the first class	Stage 2: Classes are on (supported by study)	Stage 3: SWOTVAC and exam block	Stage 4: 24 hours before an exam	Stage 5: An exam routine	Stage 6: Feedback and reflection

The key aims of reflection

There are two key strands of learning that you can have as a student:

1. The content and skills you are learning
2. Learning about how you learn

In the world of education, the second strand (learning about how you learn) is called 'metacognition'.

This book has hopefully encouraged you to think about what works best for you as a learner, whether that's in the form of flashcards, mind maps, studying in the library or at home, or in the morning or evening.

This stage of your exam experience encourages you to use feedback and reflect on what you have done well, and the areas where you can improve.

> ### Learning from students
>
> I want to go back to the survey that I did of students which identified the 'big improvers' in a high school, and the strategies and thoughts these students had on improvement.
>
> Students were given the opportunity to nominate which strategies they used to improve. The most common strategy used was 'learning from the feedback given to me (drafts, assignments and exams)', nominated by 73% of students.

Study strategies for you to use

Feedback

Learning from feedback is a study strategy that relies, in part, on students having a mindset that acknowledges that improvement is possible.

John Hattie is a well-known educational researcher who focused on the impact that different educational strategies had on student performance. One of the significant strategies in terms of positively impacting student performance is 'feedback' (Hattie, 2018). However, at times when feedback is offered, for example, when a result is released, students' reactions to the result (happiness, relief, disappointment) often dwarfs the effort to understand and learn from the feedback.

Another feedback theory that Hattie identified as important is attribution theory. While it has a grand name, it is the straightforward idea that if students attribute their good or bad results to things they have control over (like effort, organisation, use of effective study strategies), they will do better than if they attribute results to external factors (teacher, prior learning). So, as you focus on thinking about feedback, it is worth focusing on the factors you can control – on things you did well, and on things you can improve on.

Putting things into practice

The best example of feedback in practice I saw was from a hard-working Year 11 Legal Studies student. She had an exercise book that she kept in her bag, and whenever there was a practice task, peer review, draft feedback, assignment result or exam result, she would take out the exercise book and add whatever feedback had been given to her into the book. That one book had feedback for all her subjects.

This is the 'best practice' use of feedback I have seen, as it incorporates the three practical elements of feedback:

1. Pay attention to feedback as it comes; try to go beyond looking at the mark as the only feedback.
2. Acknowledge the importance of the feedback; after all, the mark can't really help you improve, but the feedback might.
3. Put together feedback from a variety of sources to look for trends in what is done well, and what can be improved.

At the very least, I would suggest that when feedback is given, you take the time to reflect on it later, when the focus is just on reading, understanding and reflecting on the feedback.

If you can go as far as the Year 11 Legal Studies student and set up a simple book to jot down all the feedback you receive, you will be in an outstanding position to learn from that feedback and improve over time.

The takeaway message

Feedback is an essential ingredient in improvement. Building a plan to be deliberate in how you use feedback will help you to improve as a student.

CHAPTER 7

The challenge of procrastination

When talking with students across different levels of ambition, one of the common challenges I come across is 'procrastination'. With a little more understanding of how effective study works, you can probably see how damaging procrastination can be, as it can:

1. Take away the chance to start early and use spaced practice
2. Force us to cram or work quickly to a deadline
3. Not give us the chance to use effective study strategies and superhabits like using practice tests/questions
4. Force us to give up the superhabit of sleep in exchange for last-minute cramming

Some fantastic ideas for challenging procrastination come from the TED talk *Inside the Mind of a Master Procrastinator* by Tim Urban (2016). In the TED talk, Urban discusses his own journey of leaving everything to the last minute.

He creates two characters that live in the brain to help understand the process of procrastination:

1. The Rational Decision-Maker – favours spreading work and effort over time
2. The Instant Gratification Monkey – enthusiastically puts off less enjoyable tasks like study to do things that are easy and fun

There is an ongoing conflict between these two – the Instant Gratification Monkey prefers to do fun things, usually prevailing over the Rational Decision-Maker's preference to get some work done.

Then there is a third character:

3. The Panic Monster – who wakes up whenever there is a deadline that is close

Importantly, the Instant Gratification Monkey is afraid of the Panic Monster.

Students can be impacted by this when they put off tasks for long periods of time – perhaps doing nothing on an assignment in the first five weeks and then spending hours working through the night to finish it the day before it is due. The Instant Gratification Monkey has, for five weeks, found enjoyable things to do instead of the assignment. However, with just one night to go, the Panic Monster takes over with the deadline close by.

Urban says the way to avoid procrastination is twofold:

1. Be aware of the Instant Gratification Monkey and the negative impact it has.
2. Be aware of time.

He suggests we set up a calendar with 90 × 52 boxes, each representing a week if we live to the age of 90. He then says:

> "We need to all take a long, hard look at that calendar. We need to think about what we're really procrastinating on, because everyone is procrastinating on something in life. We need to stay aware of the Instant Gratification Monkey. That's a job for all of us. And because there are not that many boxes on there, it's a job that should probably start today."

I can't paraphrase Urban's brilliant TED talk with the quality it deserves here; I suggest you spend 15 minutes watching it.

Battling procrastination

Here are five tips to add to your understanding of the Instant Gratification Monkey that might help you in the battle with procrastination:

1. Keep in mind the impact of the Pomodoro Technique as a simple approach to get you started on your study. Short periods of study with breaks might be easier than the challenge of trying to study for a couple of hours straight.

2. In the section on 'flow', we discussed that there is a 'hump' of effort in the first 15 to 20 minutes of work. Remember that if you can push through that, study will become easier.

3. Studying alongside other motivated students, for example, in the library, might create a positive contagion that makes it easier for you to concentrate. A library might also be an environment with a little bit of accountability (you have made the effort to go there, so you might as well get on with the study), and fewer distractions.

4. Remember the role of distraction in making learning challenging. By single-tasking when you study, you will be more efficient and find study less stressful, making it easier to do.

5. Keep your big goals in mind (for example, your future career). This is the basis of grit, perseverance toward long-term goals and making hard choices (i.e. to get started on a study session) along the way.

The takeaway message

Procrastination is a challenge. Being aware of the Instant Gratification Monkey, using the Pomodoro Technique to get started, understanding that a study session will get easier after the first 15 to 20 minutes, working alongside motivated students, keeping distractions to a minimum and keeping your big goals in mind are all tools you have to challenge tendencies around procrastination and increase study effectiveness.

Procrastination also relates to the challenge of hard choices: 'who am I to be?'. In a moment of procrastination, we have an opportunity to make a decision to take action, as we choose the person we want to be.

Finally, there are two ideas around quality study that I think challenge procrastination. The first is the acknowledgement that study impact = intensity of effort × time. And, perhaps most important of all, if you are sitting down to study, do it well. After all, life is too good for bad study.

References

Barton, D. (2015). *What do top students do differently?* TEDxYouth@Tallinn. YouTube. Retrieved 1 April 2024, from www.youtube.com/watch?v=Na8m4GPqA30

Chang, R. (2014). *How to Make Hard Choices.* TED talk. Retrieved 1 April 2024, from www.ted.com/talks/ruth_chang_how_to_make_hard_choices?language=en

Chunn, L. (2017). The psychology of the to-do list – why your brain loves ordered tasks. *The Guardian.* Retrieved 1 April 2024, from www.theguardian.com/lifeandstyle/2017/may/10/the-psychology-of-the-to-do-list-why-your-brain-loves-ordered-tasks

Damisch L., Stoberock B., & Mussweiler T. (2010). Keep your fingers crossed! How superstition improves performance. *Psychological Science, 21*(7):1014–20. doi: 10.1177/0956797610372631

Davis, S. (2020). The Secret Psychology of Why We Love Completing To-Do Lists. www.workast.com. Retrieved 7 May 2024, from www.workast.com/blog/the-secret-psychology-on-why-we-love-completing-to-do-lists

DiSalvo, D. (2018). Short Bursts of Exercise Can Give Your Brain an Edge, Study Suggests. *Forbes.* Retrieved 1 April 2024, from www.forbes.com/sites/daviddisalvo/2018/04/22/how-taking-short-exercise-breaks-can-give-your-brain-an-edge/?sh=2a329e1026fb

Duckworth, A. (2013). *Grit: The Power of Passion and Perseverance.* TED talk. Retrieved 1 April 2024, from www.ted.com/talks/angela_lee_duckworth_grit_the_power_of_passion_and_perseverance?language=en

Dunlosky, J., Rawson, K., Marsh, E., Nathan, M., & Willington, D. (2013). Improving Students' Learning with Effective Learning Techniques: Promising Directions from Cognitive and Educational Psychology. *Psychological Science in the Public Interest, 14*(1), 4–58.

Dweck, C. (2014). *The Power of Believing that you can Improve.* TED talk.

Fenesi, B., Lucibello, K., Kim, J.A., & Heisz, J.J. (2018). Sweat So You Don't Forget: Exercise Breaks During a University Lecture Increase On-Task Attention and Learning. *Journal of Applied Research in Memory and Cognition, 7*(2), 261–269.

Francis, S., & Nagel, M.C. (2023). *Your High-Performance Guide to Study and Learning: 20 Key Habits for Getting the Most Out of Your Study Time.* Amba Press.

Furber, G. (2022). Achieving the psychological state of flow. *Student Health and Wellbeing Blog at Flinders University*. Retrieved 1 April 2024, from https://blogs.flinders.edu.au/student-health-and-well-being/2022/05/02/achieving-the-psychological-state-of-flow

Furst, E. (2021). Spaced practice and its role in supporting learning and retention. *The Education Hub*. Retrieved 1 April 2024, from www.theeducationhub.org.nz/spaced-practice-and-its-role-in-supporting-learning-and-retention

Hattie, J. (2018). *Visible Learning: Feedback*. Routledge.

Hillman, C.H., Pontifex, M.B., Raine, L.B., Castelli, D.M., Hall, E.E., & Kramer, A.F. (2009). The Effect of Acute Treadmill Walking on Cognitive Control and Academic Achievement in Preadolescent Children. *Neuroscience*. 31 March; 159(3):1044–54. doi: 10.1016/j.neuroscience.2009.01.057.

Johnson. (2023). The importance of handwriting is becoming better understood. *The Economist*. Retrieved 1 April 2024, from www.economist.com/culture/2023/09/14/the-importance-of-handwriting-is-becoming-better-understood

Locke, E., & Latham, G. (2002). Building a practically useful theory of goal setting and task motivation: A 35-year odyssey. *American Psychologist, 57*(9), 705–717.

Marzano, R.J., Pickering, D.J., & Pollock, J.E. (2001). Classroom Instruction That Works. Association for Supervision and Curriculum Development.

Masicampo, E.J., & Baumeister, R.F. (2011). Consider it done! Plan making can eliminate the cognitive effects of unfulfilled goals. *Journal of Personality and Social Psychology, 101*(4), 667–683.

Murphy, M. (2018). Neuroscience Explains Why You Need to Write Down Your Goals If You Actually Want to Achieve Them. *Forbes*. Retrieved 1 April 2024, from www.forbes.com/sites/markmurphy/2018/04/15/neuroscience-explains-why-you-need-to-write-down-your-goals-if-you-actually-want-to-achieve-them/?sh=12e3093a7905

Patterson, R. (2018). The Flow State: How to Enter Your Brain's Most Productive State. *College Info Geek*. Retrieved 1 April 2024, from www.collegeinfogeek.com/flow

Paul, A.M. (2013). Multitasking While Learning. Learn. California State University, Fullerton. Retrieved 1 April 2024, from www.fullerton.edu/learn/interesting-articles/multitasking-while-studying.php

Premier Sport Psychology. (2017). Your Ticket to Successful Goal Setting. Retrieved 1 April 2024, from www.premiersportpsychology.com/2023/03/27/your-ticket-to-successful-goal-setting

Purse, M. (2024). Techniques to Tame the Fight-or-Flight Response. Verywell Mind. Retrieved 1 April 2024, from www.verywellmind.com/taming-the-fight-or-flight-response-378676

Rogers, J. (2023). Fans in awe as NBA reveals LeBron James' ridiculous four-hour pre-game routine. talkSPORT. Retrieved 1 April 2024, from www.talksport.com/sport/basketball/1667277/lebron-james-pre-game-routine

Roth, G. (n.d.). "Our Brains are Creatures of Habit". Sanitas. Retrieved 1 April 2024, from www.sanitas.com/en/magazine/living-together-today/our-brains-love-habit.html

Sekaran, K. (2023). LeBron James turns 39: Here are 3 evidence-based approaches he uses to stay fit. ABC News. Retrieved 1 April 2024, from www.abcnews.go.com/Sports/lebron-james-turns-39-evidence-based-approaches-he-uses-stay-fit/story?id=105844892

Sheff, D. (1988). 'Izzy, Did You Ask a Good Question Today?' *The New York Times*.

Swann, C. (2021). Try setting an open goal for your New Year's resolution if you want to exercise more. ABC News. Retrieved 1 April 2024, from www.abc.net.au/news/2021-01-01/new-years-resolution-goals-should-be-open-not-specific/13017290

Turgeon, H., & Wright, J. (2022). *Generation Sleepless: Why Tweens and Teens Aren't Sleeping Enough and How We Can Help Them*. TarcherPerigee.

Urban, T. (2016). *Inside the Mind of a Master Procrastinator*. TED. Retrieved 1 April 2024, from www.ted.com/talks/tim_urban_inside_the_mind_of_a_master_procrastinator

www.ingramcontent.com/pod-product-compliance
Lightning Source LLC
Chambersburg PA
CBHW070318120526
44590CB00017B/2731